THIS IS A SITUATIONAL BOOK TO PROMOTE PROBLEM-SOLVING SKILLS AMONG YOUNG CHILDREN. OPEN-ENDED DISCUSSIONS WITH ADULT GUIDANCE ARE ENCOURAGED.

IT IS MEANT TO BE USED ONE-ON-ONE OR IN GROUP SETTINGS.

WHAT WOULD YOU DO IF...

SOMEONE MAKES FUN OF YOU?

WHAT WOULD YOU DO IF...

SOMEONE SAID SOMETHING ABOUT YOU THAT ISN'T TRUE?

WHAT WOULD YOU DO IF...

SOMEBODY HIT YOU?

WHAT WOULD YOU DO IF...

SOMEONE TOOK SOMETHING FROM YOU AND DIDN'T WANT TO GIVE IT BACK?

WHAT WOULD YOU DO IF...

NO ONE WANTED TO SIT WITH YOU AT LUNCH OR RECESS?

WHAT WOULD YOU DO IF...

SOMEONE MADE FUN OF YOUR BODY?

WHAT WOULD YOU DO IF...

SOMEONE WAS SITTING ALL ALONE AND LOOKED SAD?

WHAT WOULD YOU DO IF...

SOMEONE LIED TO YOU?

WHAT ARE SOME THINGS THAT HAPPEN WHEN YOU ARE WITH YOUR FRIENDS THAT YOU LIKE OR DON'T LIKE?

How do you feel
when something you don't
like happens?

Why?

How do you feel when something you like happens?

Why?

CAN YOU REMEMBER SOMETHING
YOU DID ALL BY YOURSELF?

HOW DID THAT MAKE YOU FEEL?

I WISH TO DEDICATE THIS BOOK
TO MY FATHER, "GENNAR' U MASTONE".

YOU MADE EVERYONE SMILE.

NOTES